This book belongs to:

_____

To Javi, Lara, and Alex.
M.A.E

To my parents,
Néstor and Ana.
S.R.A.

Special thanks to all the Kickstarter backers and the Messy Supporter Laura Mallol.
Thanks to Sarah Ward, Maria Bustos, Simona Manca, and Rene Chan for their feedback.

www.MartaAlmansa.com
@martaalmansabooks

Copyright © 2023 Marta Almansa Esteva
Illustrations by Silvia Romeral Andrés
First published 2023
Paperback ISBN: 978-1-915193-08-7
Hardcover ISBN: 978-1-915193-09-4

HERE comes the MESS

Marta Almansa Esteva

Silvia Romeral Andrés

Have you ever wondered how messy a mess can get?
I'm not talking about getting a little bit dirty
here and there. I'm talking about serious,
all-over-the-place mess.

Meet my brother, Rob.
He's six months old and can sit by himself. And believe me,
he wants to eat. He's been watching all of us eating
for months when he was only allowed milk.

My mum says it's safe for Rob to start eating the same food we eat. He will explore food and learn to feed himself at his own pace.

Rob probably thinks his tummy is
as big as a dinosaur's and
that all the food will fit in there.
I'm sure his stomach is
not that big.

But anyway, that's not the real trouble.
The real issue here is the mess.
Oh, the mess!

What's a little spill here and there?
That's mess for beginners.
Let me tell you about Rob's
professional-level mess.

We were having lunch the other day,
and Rob started throwing spaghetti at the wall.
One, two, three handfuls of spaghetti
went flying and got stuck!

But that wasn't all. He then decided
that adding some tomato
sauce was a great idea.
He threw some of that too.

Another day, we were having a snack:
yoghurt with strawberries.

Soon, Rob ended up looking like **Santa!** He had a white yoghurt beard and red strawberries on top of his head.

My mum cooked us some **giant pasta** one evening. That was cool!

It was so cool that Rob decided the pasta was a
shaker. He started playing songs while
the pasta flew around the room.

My dad loves bananas.
He eats so many so often that
I'm sure he would love to be a monkey.

When Rob tries new foods for the first time,
his faces are just the funniest!
I don't think Rob is **a big fan of bananas**.
That means more for my daddy!

Rob has a cup for drinking water.
When he's not thirsty, it can be a problem.

He loves pretending to be a firefighter with a water hose.
That is a **really wet kind of mess**.

You see, eating with Rob can be a bit messy sometimes. That's why he wears a bib when he eats.

One day, we forgot to put his bib on for breakfast. We found cereal between his toes, on his ears, and in his nappy. That was **not a fun sight**.

Rob doesn't know how to use a spoon yet.
He plays with it like a xylophone.
He has a go at throwing it and
seeing where it lands.

It may land on top of the fridge or in the cat's food bowl. **You never know.**

The **messiest mess** usually happens when Rob has porridge or rice. The tiny bits of food seem to be playing hide-and-seek, and they always end up in weird places.

In Mummy's pockets. In Daddy's shoes. On my nose. **Nowhere is safe** when Rob is around and making a mess.

Every day, Rob is learning how to eat, what he likes, and what he's not too sure about yet. It's made me realise that eating is **hard work**. We all have to learn at some point.

It's so much fun having Rob eat
with us at the table.
He might be messy,
but **I love him so much!**

My parents say I was messy when I started eating too.
But look at me now! I'm a **big girl**.

I use my fork and spoon. I eat all sorts of
food, and I make almost no mess!
Rob just needs time and practice,
and we'll **enjoy the fun** until then!

What's your favourite kind of mess?

very wet mess

'this is a disaster' mess

tiny type of mess

unexpected mess

all-over-the-place mess

fruity mess

Can you spot your favourite mess in the book?

Did you enjoy this book? Please leave a review!
And if you did... I've got a little gift for you! Thanks so much for your support! Claim your gift at martaalmansa.com/messy-gift

Printed in the USA
CPSIA information can be obtained
at www.ICGtesting.com
LVHW060745260124
769968LV00005B/77

9 781915 193094